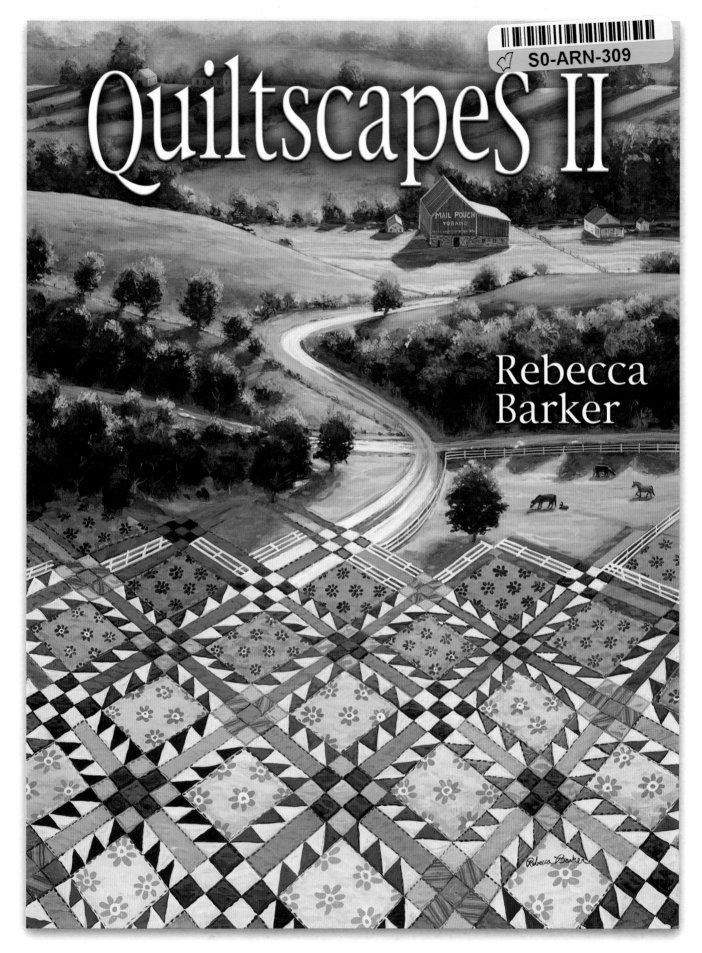

Quiltscapes II

Rebecca Barker

American Quilter's Society

P. O. Box 3290 • Paducah, KY 42002-3290

www.AmericanQuilter.com

Located in Paducah, Kentucky, the American Quilter's Society (AQS) is dedicated to promoting the accomplishments of today's quilters. Through its publications and events, AQS strives to honor today's quilt-makers and their work and to inspire future creativity and innovation in quiltmaking.

EDITOR: BARBARA SMITH
GRAPHIC DESIGN: ELAINE WILSON
COVER DESIGN: MICHAEL BUCKINGHAM

Library of Congress Cataloging-in-Publication Data
Barker, Rebecca.
      Quiltscapes II / by Rebecca Barker
         p. cm.
      Summary: "Full-page photos of acrylic paintings of traditional quilts integrated into landscapes, seascapes, still lifes and farm scenes. Instructions for block patterns include Vermont Maple Leaf, Poppy, Prairie Flower, Dove in the Window, Lady of the Lake, Windblown Star, Waves of the Sea, Flower Basket and more"--Provided by publisher.
      Includes bibliographical references.
      ISBN 1-57432-878-6
      1. Patchwork--Patterns. 2. Appliqué--Patterns. 3. Quilting--Patterns. I. Title: Quiltscapes 2. II. Title.
      TT835.B266523 2005
      746.46'041--dc22
                        2004027717

Additional copies of this book may be ordered from the American Quilter's Society, PO Box 3290, Paducah, KY 42002-3290; 800-626-5420 (orders only please); or online at www.AmericanQuilter.com. For all other inquiries, call 270-898-7903.

(on the title page)
KENTUCKY CROSSROADS
I created this painting of a landscape characteristic of eastern Kentucky. Kentucky is only a few miles from my Cincinnati home.

Dedication

In memory of my beloved father,

Charles W. Barker

Roses

*This is a multi-patterned appliquéd quilt composed of some of the
first rose blocks ever created.*

Pennsylvania Dutch

The old stone houses and beautiful hex symbol barns I see in Pennsylvania inspired this painting.

Contents

Introduction

The first *Quiltscapes* book received so many requests for more pictures and patterns that a second one was inevitable. The author, Rebecca Barker, hopes it will bring you many hours of happy quilting and much joy as you look at her landscape paintings and make these beautiful blocks.

Rebecca invented the word "quiltscapes" for these paintings that depict the titles of old-time quilt block patterns. These acrylic paintings on masonite board have a realistic style with an emphasis on color, clarity, and composition. People often come up to her work and touch the surface because they think she glued a quilt onto the painting. She says it's a great compliment when they do that.

In the following pages, each of the beautiful quilt paintings depicts a pattern of one or more quilt blocks. Rotary-cutting measurements are given for those patches that can be rotary cut. Full-sized patterns are provided for those patches that do not lend themselves to rotary cutting. For the appliqué blocks, you will need to add ³⁄₁₆" turn-under allowances to the patch patterns. For the pieced blocks, add ¼" allowances.

For your convenience in planning your projects, the block patterns are accompanied by charts to help you determine how many pieces can be cut from a fat quarter. Select scraps for the smaller appliqué pieces.

Try combining like-sized blocks in your quilts for added excitement. Some of the blocks will be quite easy to sew for those who are familiar with basic quiltmaking techniques. Several of the blocks may be more challenging, even for experienced quilters.

Block Patterns

Rising Sun

This was the fourth quiltscape I painted, and it remains one of my favorites because I love the pattern. I don't own the quilts I paint. They do not exist because I make them up to match the landscapes.

Lady of the Lake

Lady of the Lake

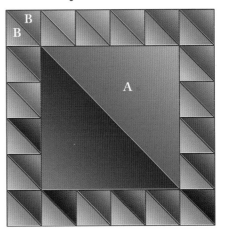

LADY OF THE LAKE

If you turn the picture upside down, you can see the reflection of the lady in the lake.

12" FINISHED BLOCK
Pieces in a fat quarter (18" x 20")
8 A
72 B

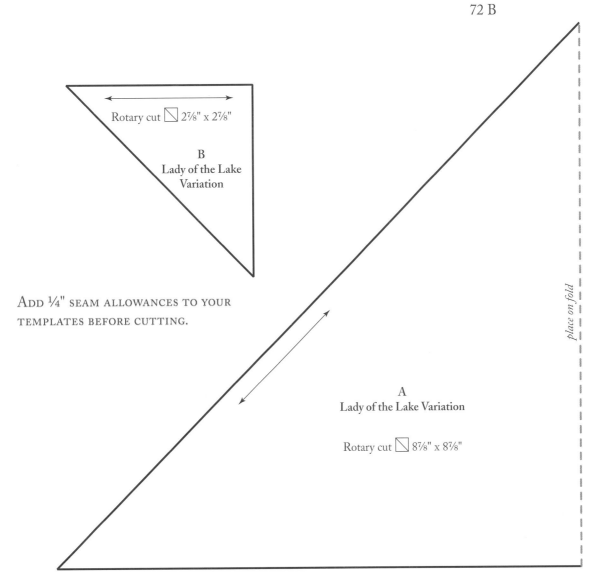

Rotary cut ◻ 2⅞" x 2⅞"

B
Lady of the Lake
Variation

ADD ¼" SEAM ALLOWANCES TO YOUR TEMPLATES BEFORE CUTTING.

A
Lady of the Lake Variation

Rotary cut ◻ 8⅞" x 8⅞"

place on fold

Cardinals

Cardinals

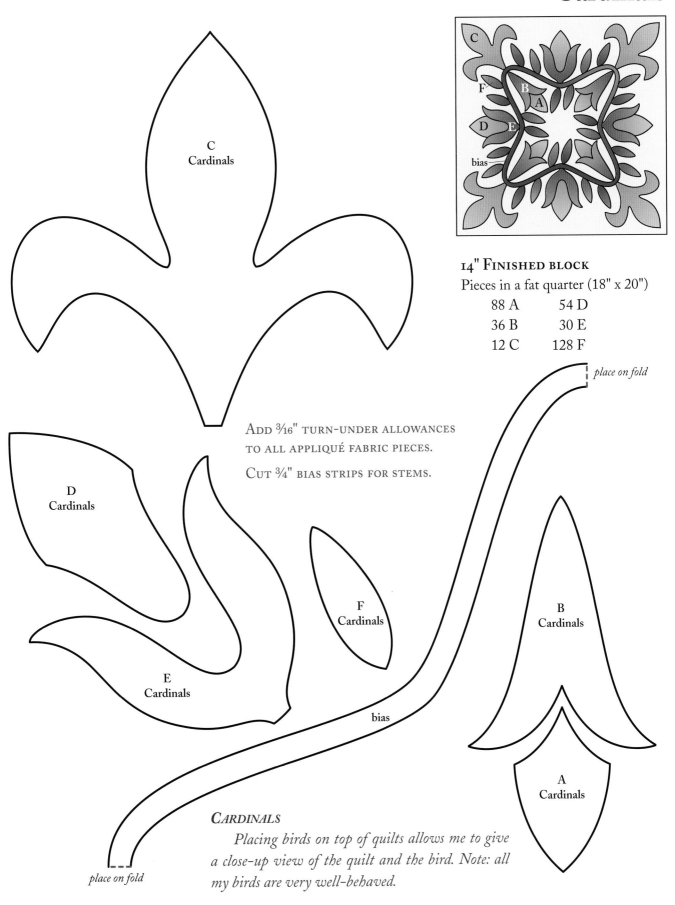

C
Cardinals

14" FINISHED BLOCK

Pieces in a fat quarter (18" x 20")

88 A	54 D
36 B	30 E
12 C	128 F

place on fold

ADD ³⁄₁₆" TURN-UNDER ALLOWANCES
TO ALL APPLIQUÉ FABRIC PIECES.

CUT ¾" BIAS STRIPS FOR STEMS.

D
Cardinals

F
Cardinals

B
Cardinals

E
Cardinals

bias

A
Cardinals

place on fold

CARDINALS

*Placing birds on top of quilts allows me to give
a close-up view of the quilt and the bird. Note: all
my birds are very well-behaved.*

Airplane

I rarely make up or alter quilt patterns, but this airplane block is a mixture of several patterns that are similar.

Rebecca Barker

Airplane

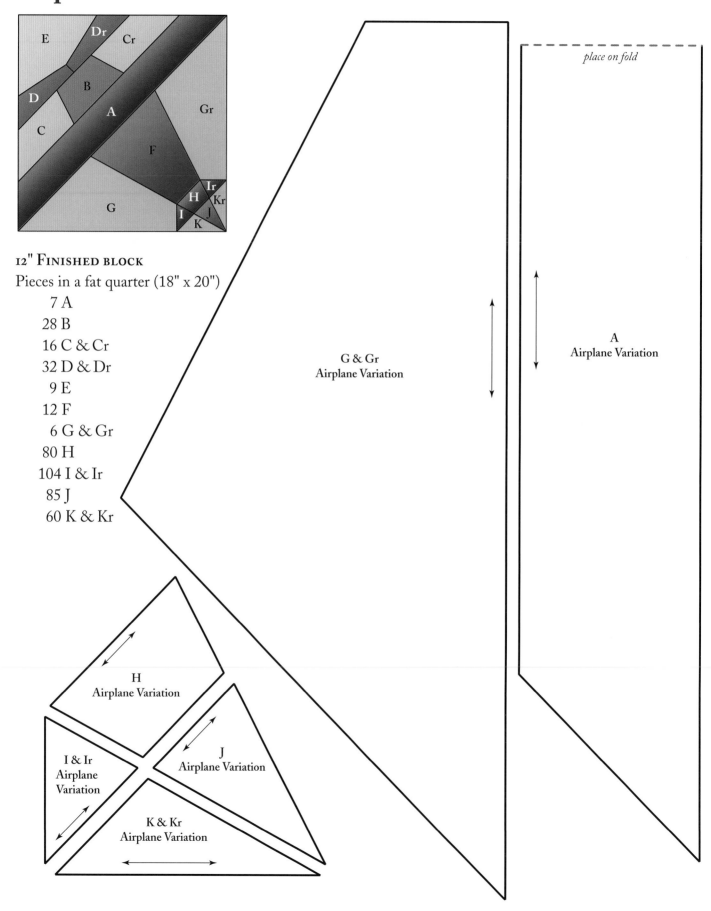

12" Finished block

Pieces in a fat quarter (18" x 20")

- 7 A
- 28 B
- 16 C & Cr
- 32 D & Dr
- 9 E
- 12 F
- 6 G & Gr
- 80 H
- 104 I & Ir
- 85 J
- 60 K & Kr

G & Gr
Airplane Variation

place on fold

A
Airplane Variation

H
Airplane Variation

I & Ir
Airplane
Variation

J
Airplane Variation

K & Kr
Airplane Variation

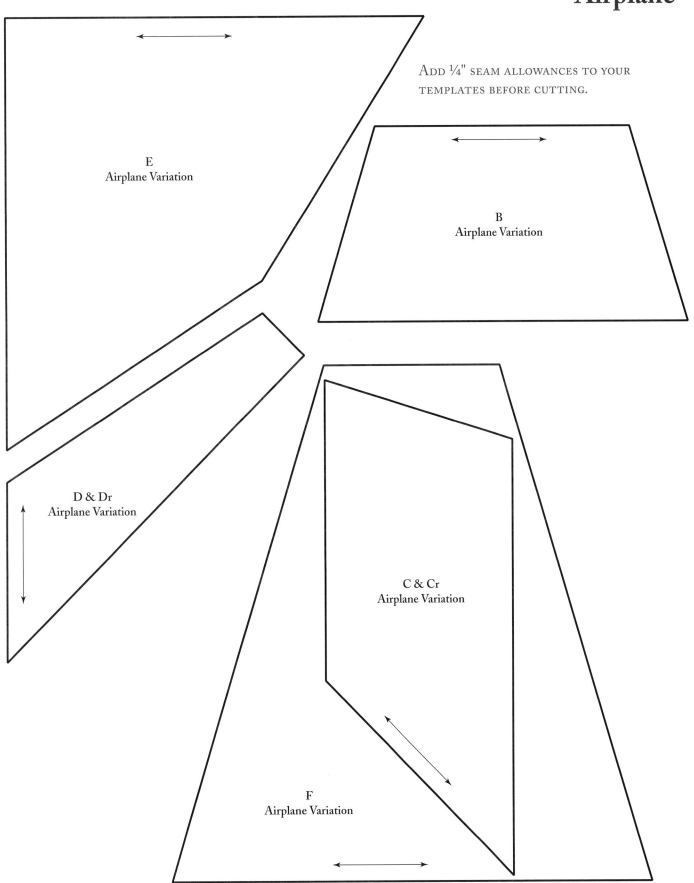

Airplane

E
Airplane Variation

Add ¼" seam allowances to your templates before cutting.

B
Airplane Variation

D & Dr
Airplane Variation

C & Cr
Airplane Variation

F
Airplane Variation

Delectable Mountain

Delectable Mountain

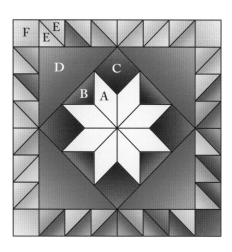

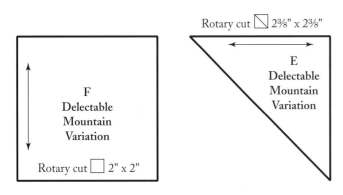

Rotary cut ⬜ 2⅜" x 2⅜"

E
Delectable
Mountain
Variation

F
Delectable
Mountain
Variation

Rotary cut ⬜ 2" x 2"

A𝐃𝐃 ¼" 𝐬𝐞𝐚𝐦 𝐚𝐥𝐥𝐨𝐰𝐚𝐧𝐜𝐞𝐬 𝐭𝐨 𝐲𝐨𝐮𝐫
𝐭𝐞𝐦𝐩𝐥𝐚𝐭𝐞𝐬 𝐛𝐞𝐟𝐨𝐫𝐞 𝐜𝐮𝐭𝐭𝐢𝐧𝐠.

12" F𝐈𝐍𝐈𝐒𝐇𝐄𝐃 𝐁𝐋𝐎𝐂𝐊
Pieces in a fat quarter (18" x 20")

45 A	18 D
80 B	112 E
56 C	90 F

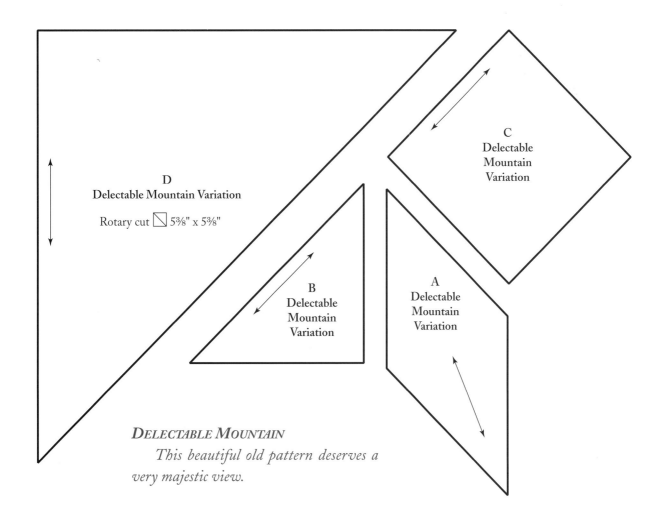

D
Delectable Mountain Variation

Rotary cut ⬜ 5⅜" x 5⅜"

C
Delectable
Mountain
Variation

B
Delectable
Mountain
Variation

A
Delectable
Mountain
Variation

D𝐄𝐋𝐄𝐂𝐓𝐀𝐁𝐋𝐄 M𝐎𝐔𝐍𝐓𝐀𝐈𝐍
*This beautiful old pattern deserves a
very majestic view.*

Chickadees

Chickadees

CHICKADEES

I do bird watching as a hobby. It refreshes my spirit and allows me to connect with nature.

ADD ³⁄₁₆" TURN-UNDER ALLOWANCES TO ALL APPLIQUÉ FABRIC PIECES.

CUT ¾" BIAS STRIPS FOR STEMS.

place on fold

place on fold

A
Chickadees

G
Chickadees

B
Chickadees

C
Chickadees

D
Chickadees

E/Er
Chickadees

F
Chickadees

14" FINISHED BLOCK
Pieces in a fat quarter (18" x 20")
  4 A

Cut small appliqué pieces B–F from scraps.

Wind Blown Star

I tried to depict a stormy and windy day by using dark colors in this painting, but the light beam makes it a happier picture.

Wind Blown Star

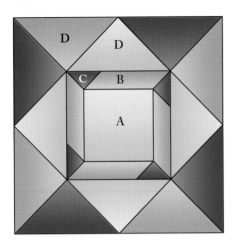

12" FINISHED BLOCK

Pieces in a fat quarter (18" x 20")

     16 A

     35 B

     120 C

     16 D

A
Wind Blown Star Variation

Rotary cut ▢ 4½" x 4½"

D
Wind Blown Star Variation

Rotary cut ⊠ 7¼" x 7¼"

B
Wind Blown Star Variation

ADD ¼" SEAM ALLOWANCES TO YOUR TEMPLATES BEFORE CUTTING.

Rotary cut ⊠ 3¼" x 3¼"

C
Wind Blown Star Variation

Dove in the Window

Dove in the Window

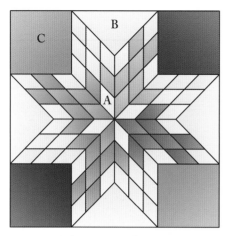

DOVE IN THE WINDOW

This pattern has many names, but I used Dove in the Window to depict my two loves, flowers and birds.

12" FINISHED BLOCK

Pieces in a fat quarter (18" x 20")

84 A

24 B

20 C

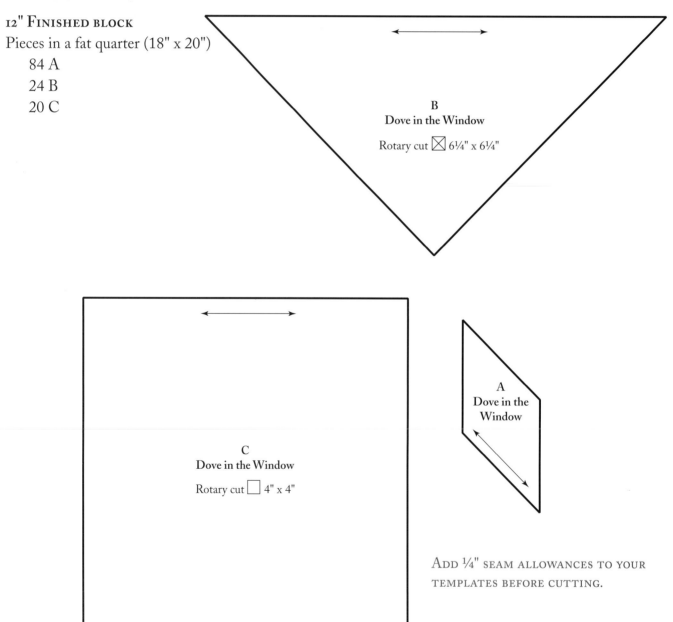

B
Dove in the Window

Rotary cut ⊠ 6¼" x 6¼"

C
Dove in the Window

Rotary cut ☐ 4" x 4"

A
Dove in the Window

ADD ¼" SEAM ALLOWANCES TO YOUR TEMPLATES BEFORE CUTTING.

County Fair

When I was very young, I participated in 4H with my pony. I would go to the county fair every summer. I feel this pattern expresses my memories and the movement, action, and colors of the fair.

County Fair

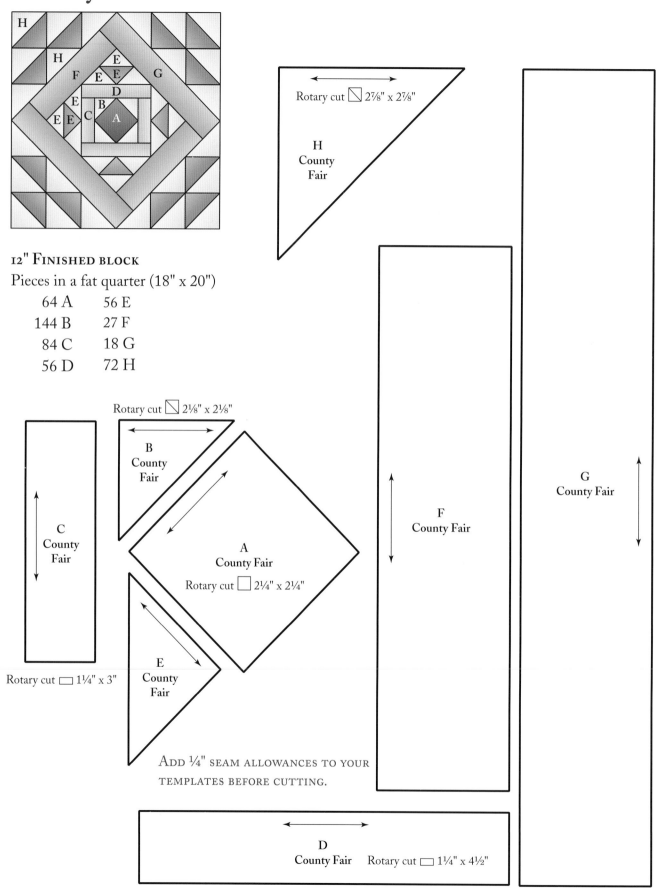

12" Finished block
Pieces in a fat quarter (18" x 20")

64 A	56 E
144 B	27 F
84 C	18 G
56 D	72 H

H
County Fair
Rotary cut ⬜ 2⅞" x 2⅞"

B
County Fair
Rotary cut ◺ 2⅛" x 2⅛"

C
County Fair
Rotary cut ▭ 1¼" x 3"

A
County Fair
Rotary cut ⬜ 2¼" x 2¼"

E
County Fair

F
County Fair

G
County Fair

ADD ¼" SEAM ALLOWANCES TO YOUR
TEMPLATES BEFORE CUTTING.

D
County Fair   Rotary cut ▭ 1¼" x 4½"

Melon Patch

Melon Patch

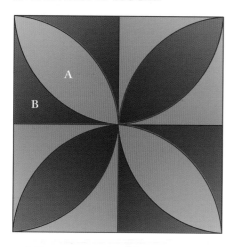

12" FINISHED BLOCK

Pieces in a fat quarter (18" x 20")

    8 A

    6 B

MELON PATCH

This quilt pattern has many other names. I wanted to paint a watermelon field, so I found this pattern to go with it.

ADD ¼" SEAM ALLOWANCES TO YOUR TEMPLATES BEFORE CUTTING.

ADD ³⁄₁₆" TURN-UNDER ALLOWANCES TO ALL APPLIQUÉ FABRIC PIECES.

A
Melon Patch

B
Melon Patch

Rotary cut ▢ 6½" x 6½"

Sunflowers

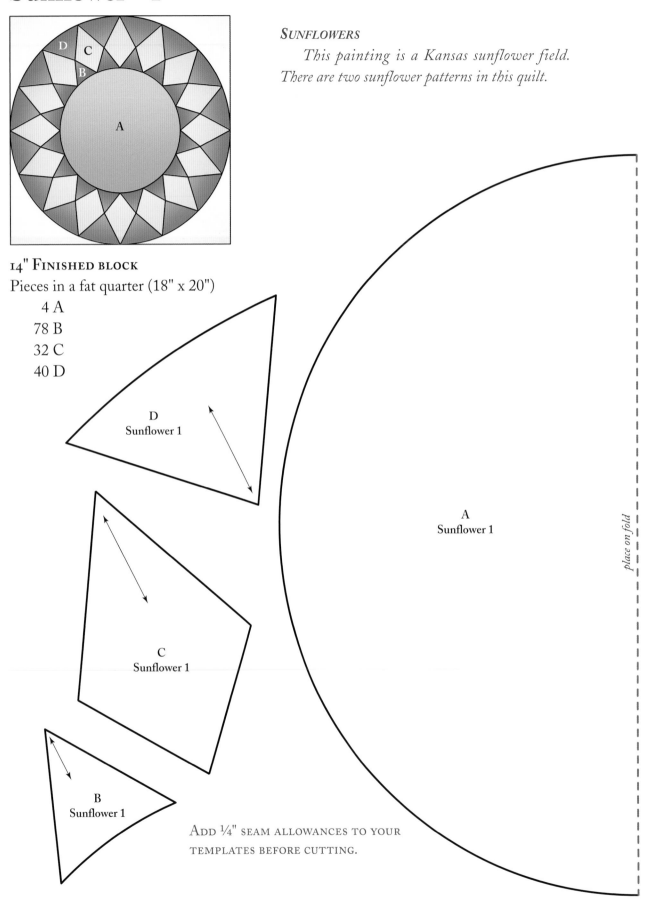

Sunflower – I

SUNFLOWERS

This painting is a Kansas sunflower field.
There are two sunflower patterns in this quilt.

14" FINISHED BLOCK

Pieces in a fat quarter (18" x 20")

4 A
78 B
32 C
40 D

D
Sunflower 1

C
Sunflower 1

B
Sunflower 1

A
Sunflower 1

place on fold

ADD ¼" SEAM ALLOWANCES TO YOUR
TEMPLATES BEFORE CUTTING.

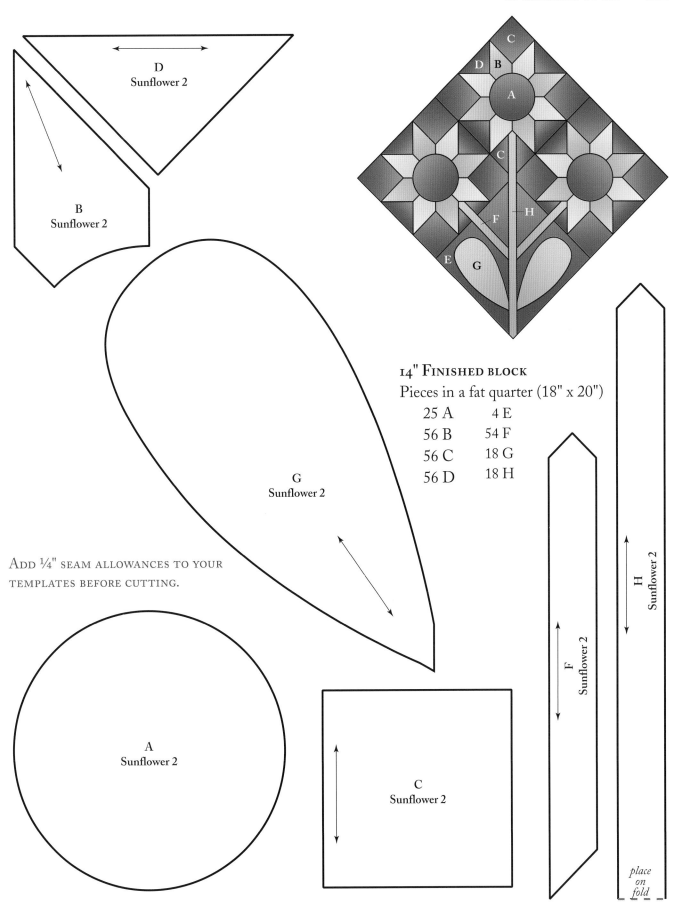

Sunflower – II

D
Sunflower 2

B
Sunflower 2

G
Sunflower 2

14" Finished block

Pieces in a fat quarter (18" x 20")

25 A	4 E
56 B	54 F
56 C	18 G
56 D	18 H

Add ¼" seam allowances to your templates before cutting.

A
Sunflower 2

C
Sunflower 2

F
Sunflower 2

H
Sunflower 2

place on fold

Sunflower – II

←—————→

ADD ¼" SEAM ALLOWANCES TO YOUR
TEMPLATES BEFORE CUTTING.

E
Sunflower 2

Rotary cut ☐ 7½" x 7½"

Poppy

Poppy

Add 3/16" turn-under allowances to all appliqué fabric pieces.

Cut 3/4" bias strips for stems.

Poppy

ADD ³⁄₁₆" TURN-UNDER ALLOWANCES
TO ALL APPLIQUÉ FABRIC PIECES.

CUT ¾" BIAS STRIPS FOR STEMS.

POPPY

*This pattern is a Marie Webster design
from 1912. I have been to her home that is
now a museum. Her quilts are so beautiful, I
had to use one in this poppy landscape.*

18" FINISHED BLOCK
Use scraps for these small appliqué pieces.

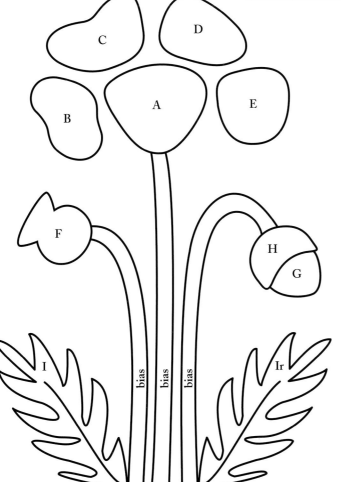

6" FINISHED BORDER
Use scraps for these small appliqué pieces.

Cactus Flower Pot

My sister lives in the Southwest, and I visit her regularly. We took a trip to the cactus area in Arizona, and I fell in love with that part of the country.

Cactus Flower Pot

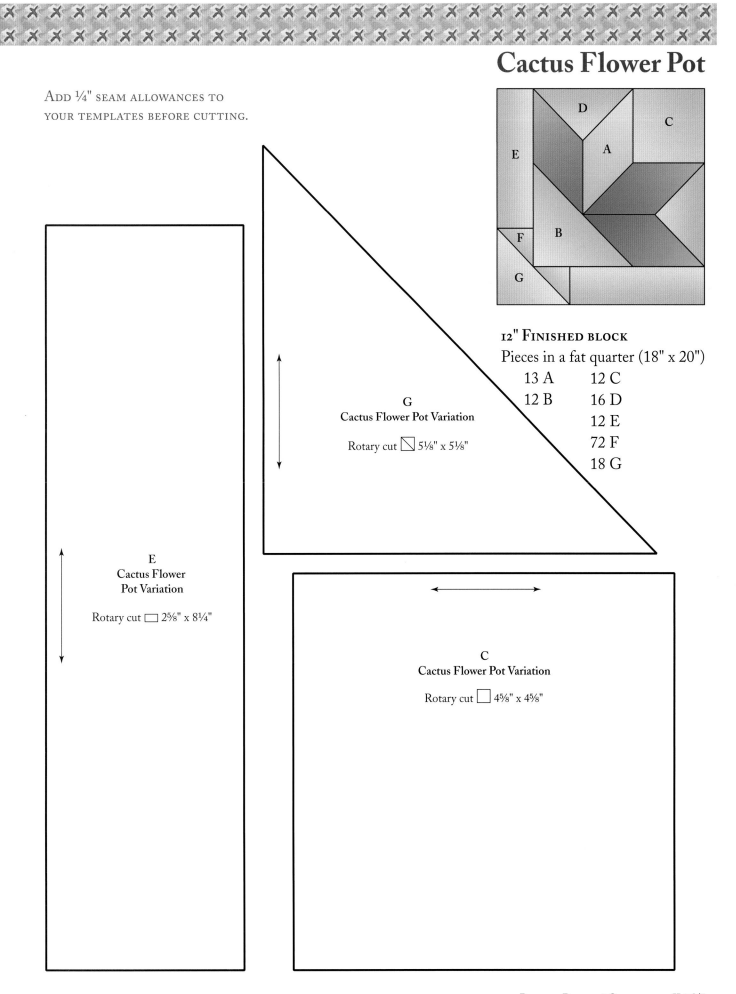

ADD ¼" SEAM ALLOWANCES TO
YOUR TEMPLATES BEFORE CUTTING.

12" FINISHED BLOCK
Pieces in a fat quarter (18" x 20")

13 A	12 C
12 B	16 D
	12 E
	72 F
	18 G

G
Cactus Flower Pot Variation

Rotary cut ◻ 5⅛" x 5⅛"

E
Cactus Flower
Pot Variation

Rotary cut ▭ 2⅝" x 8¼"

C
Cactus Flower Pot Variation

Rotary cut ◻ 4⅝" x 4⅝"

Cactus Flower Pot

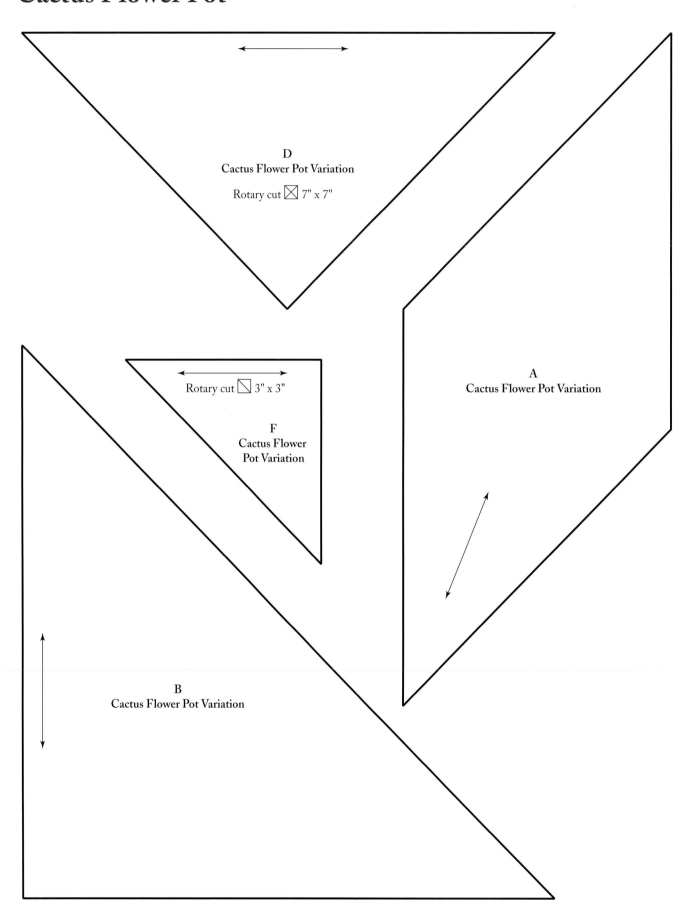

D
Cactus Flower Pot Variation

Rotary cut ⊠ 7" x 7"

Rotary cut ◪ 3" x 3"

F
Cactus Flower
Pot Variation

A
Cactus Flower Pot Variation

B
Cactus Flower Pot Variation

Acorns & Oak Leaves

*There is a chipmunk that lives under my front porch, and he inspired me to paint
him with a quilt. I found this quilt block pattern which goes well with his lifestyle.*

C
Acorns & Oak Leaves

Rotary cut ⬜ 1¾" x 14½"

place on fold

Acorns & Oak Leaves

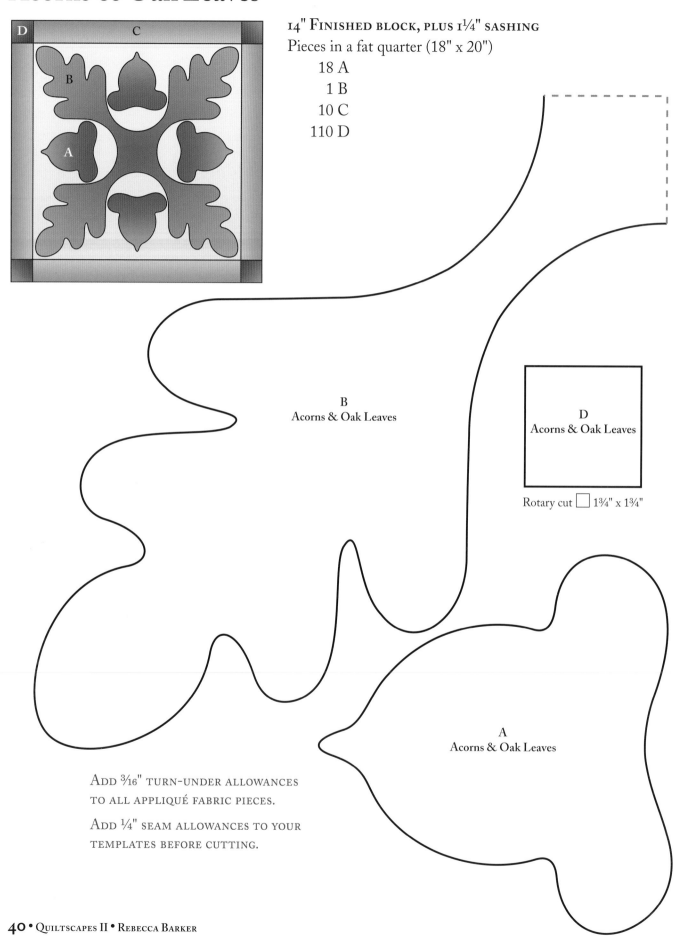

14" Finished block, plus 1¼" sashing
Pieces in a fat quarter (18" x 20")

18 A
1 B
10 C
110 D

B
Acorns & Oak Leaves

D
Acorns & Oak Leaves

Rotary cut ▢ 1¾" x 1¾"

A
Acorns & Oak Leaves

Add ³⁄₁₆" turn-under allowances
to all appliqué fabric pieces.

Add ¼" seam allowances to your
templates before cutting.

Farmer's Field

Farmer's Field

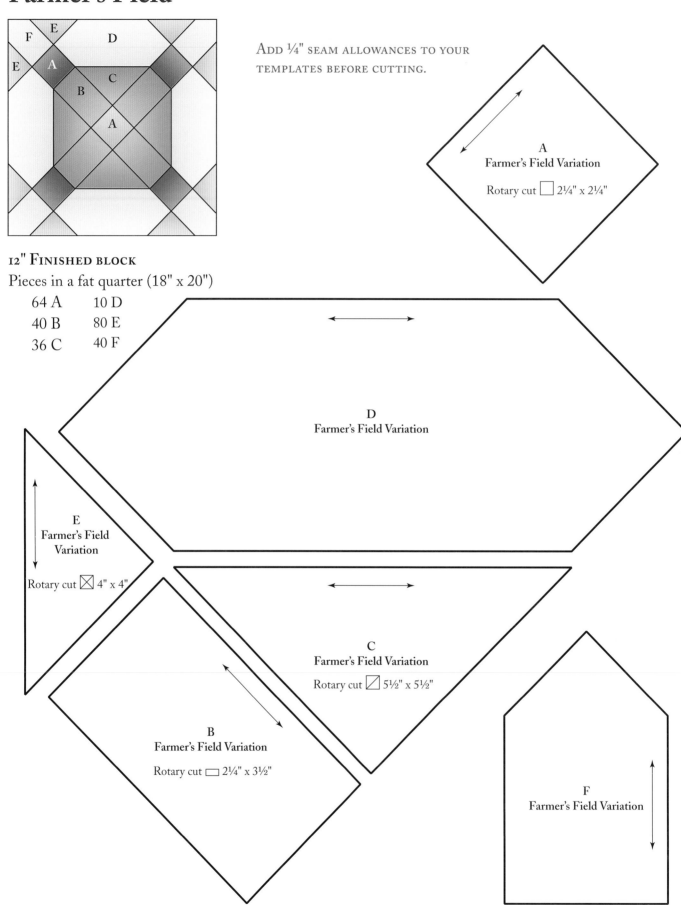

ADD ¼" SEAM ALLOWANCES TO YOUR
TEMPLATES BEFORE CUTTING.

A
Farmer's Field Variation

Rotary cut ☐ 2¼" x 2¼"

12" **FINISHED BLOCK**

Pieces in a fat quarter (18" x 20")

64 A	10 D
40 B	80 E
36 C	40 F

D
Farmer's Field Variation

E
Farmer's Field
Variation

Rotary cut ⊠ 4" x 4"

C
Farmer's Field Variation

Rotary cut ◺ 5½" x 5½"

B
Farmer's Field Variation

Rotary cut ▭ 2¼" x 3½"

F
Farmer's Field Variation

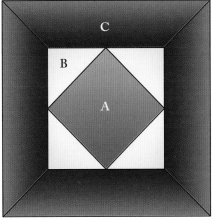

ADD ¼" SEAM ALLOWANCES TO
YOUR TEMPLATES BEFORE CUTTING.

A
Farmer's Field

Rotary cut ⬜ 5¼" x 5¼"

12" FINISHED BLOCK
Pieces in a fat quarter (18" x 20")
9 A
32 B
5 C

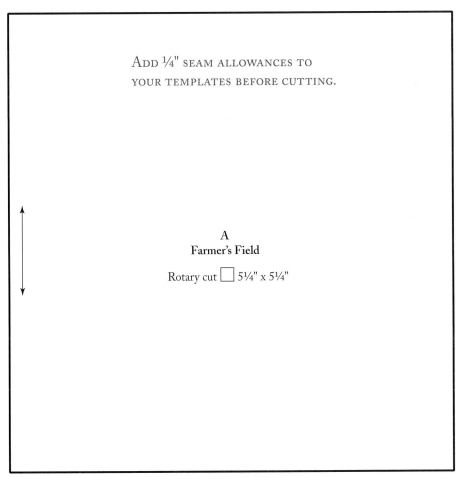

FARMER'S FIELD

*My paintings that depict the quilt on the land
are harder to design. It is worth the effort though,
because they are a lot of fun to look at.*

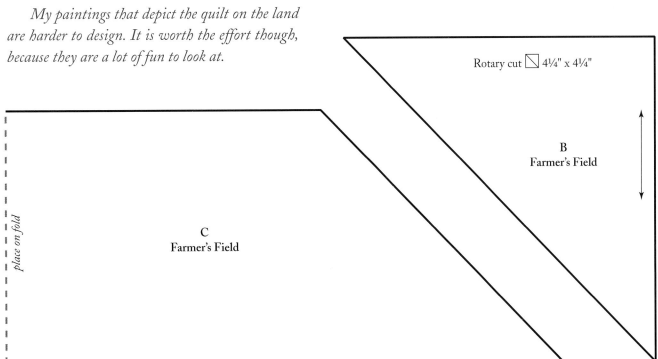

Rotary cut ◹ 4¼" x 4¼"

B
Farmer's Field

place on fold

C
Farmer's Field

Vermont Maple Leaf

Vermont Maple Leaf

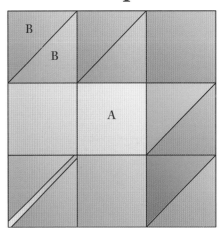

VERMONT MAPLE LEAF

    I have attended the Vermont Quilt Festival and love the small towns with their little white churches.

9" FINISHED BLOCK

Pieces in a fat quarter (18" x 20")

    25 A

    40 B

ADD ¼" SEAM ALLOWANCES TO YOUR TEMPLATES BEFORE CUTTING.

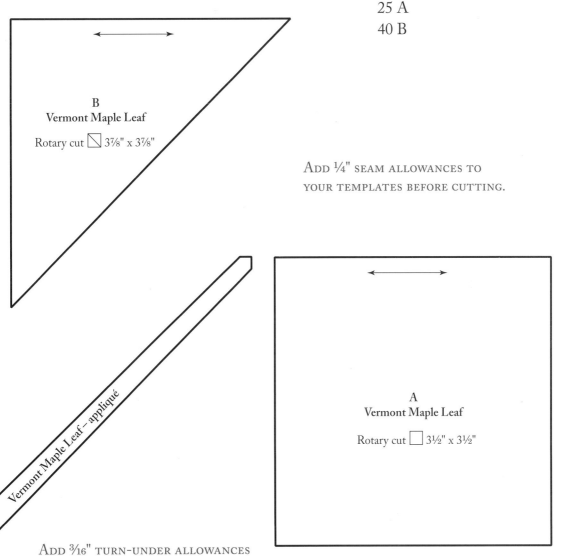

B
Vermont Maple Leaf

Rotary cut ⬜ 3⅞" x 3⅞"

Vermont Maple Leaf – appliqué

A
Vermont Maple Leaf

Rotary cut ⬜ 3½" x 3½"

ADD ³⁄₁₆" TURN-UNDER ALLOWANCES TO ALL APPLIQUÉ FABRIC PIECES.

Prairie Flower

This is a very old and lovely appliqué pattern called Prairie Flower. Look for a prairie dog in the middle.

Prairie Flower

N
Prairie
Flower

Rotary cut □ 1¾" x 1¾"

14" **Finished block, plus** 1¼" **sashing**

Pieces in a fat quarter (18" x 20")

Use scraps for the smaller appliqué pieces.

    20 B
    12 C
    10 M
  100 N

M
sashing

Prairie
Flower

Rotary cut ▯
1¾" x 14½"

Add ¼" seam allowances to
your templates before cutting.

place on fold

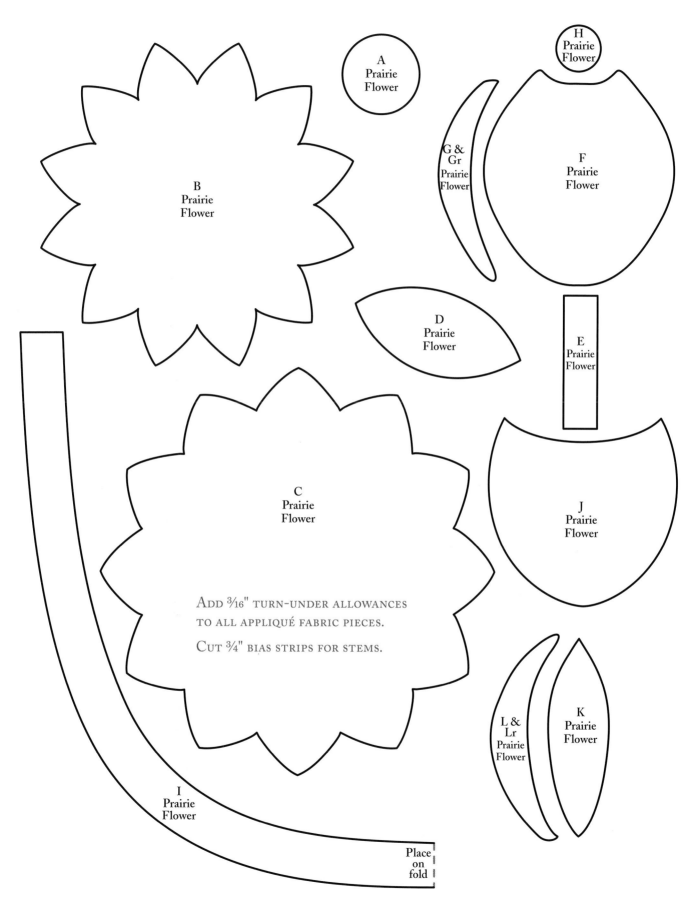

Add ³⁄₁₆" turn-under allowances to all appliqué fabric pieces.

Cut ¾" bias strips for stems.

Pumpkin Vine

Pumpkin Vine

12" Finished block
Pieces in a fat quarter (18" x 20")
12 A
6 B

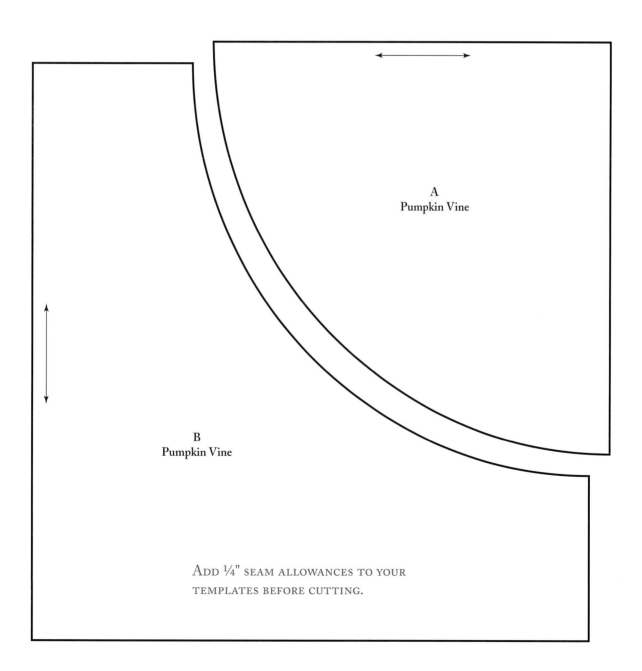

PUMPKIN VINE

This pattern has many names, but I used the pumpkin vine to depict a scene I saw in northern Ohio where the Amish were selling their pumpkins by the side of the road.

A
Pumpkin Vine

B
Pumpkin Vine

ADD ¼" SEAM ALLOWANCES TO YOUR TEMPLATES BEFORE CUTTING.

Waves of the Sea

This painting subtly shows the quilt pattern Waves of the Sea in the wave. There is a small light-house in the distance that is on Cape Cod. Pattern on page 54.

Waves of the Sea

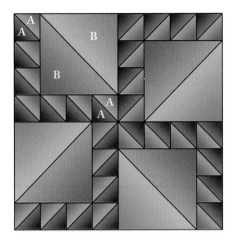

Quilt photo on pages 52 and 53.

ADD ¼" SEAM ALLOWANCES TO YOUR
TEMPLATES BEFORE CUTTING.

12" FINISHED BLOCK
Pieces in a fat quarter (18" x 20")

    112 A
     18 B

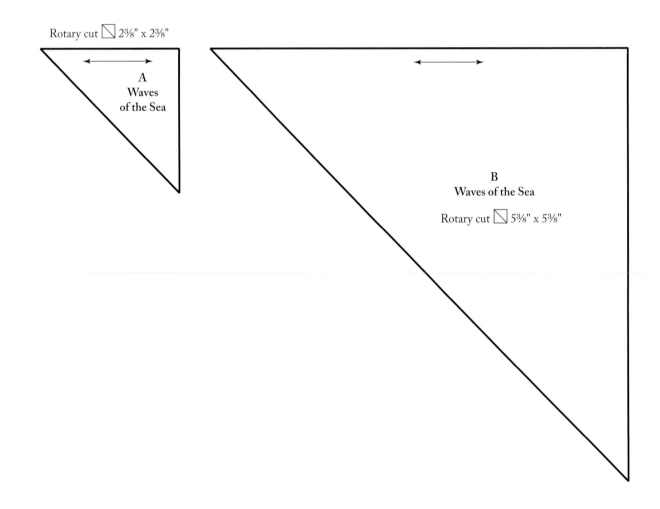

Rotary cut ◻ 2⅜" x 2⅜"

A
Waves
of the Sea

B
Waves of the Sea

Rotary cut ◻ 5⅜" x 5⅜"

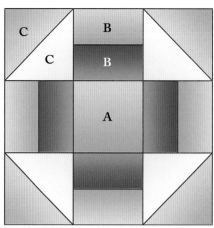

Quilt photo on pages 56 and 57.

ADD ¼" SEAM ALLOWANCES TO YOUR TEMPLATES BEFORE CUTTING.

9" FINISHED BLOCK
Pieces in a fat quarter (18" x 20")
25 A
45 B
40 C

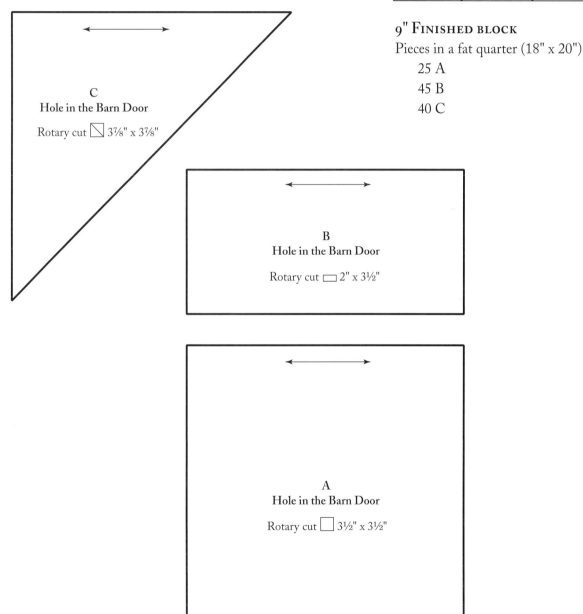

C
Hole in the Barn Door

Rotary cut 3⅞" x 3⅞"

B
Hole in the Barn Door

Rotary cut 2" x 3½"

A
Hole in the Barn Door

Rotary cut 3½" x 3½"

Hole in the Barn Door

The name of this quilt pattern fits the design well. It is difficult to see, but there is a cow looking out of the hole in the barn door. Pattern on page 55.

Milky Way

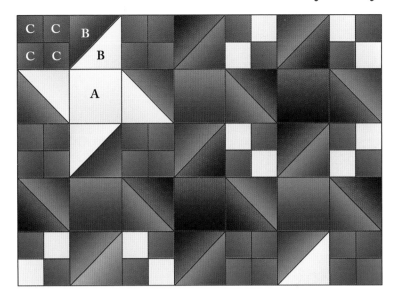

MILKY WAY

The many tiny stars in this quilted sky reflect the Milky Way below.

9" FINISHED BLOCK

Pieces in a fat quarter (18" x 20")

- 25 A
- 40 B
- 90 C

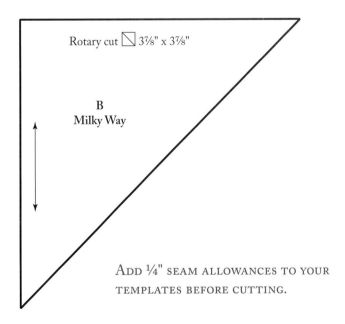

C
Milky Way

Rotary cut ▢ 2" x 2"

B
Milky Way

Rotary cut ◹ 3⅞" x 3⅞"

ADD ¼" SEAM ALLOWANCES TO YOUR TEMPLATES BEFORE CUTTING.

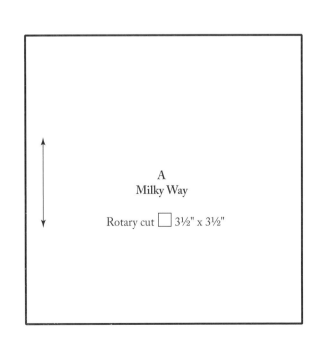

A
Milky Way

Rotary cut ▢ 3½" x 3½"

Bear's Paw

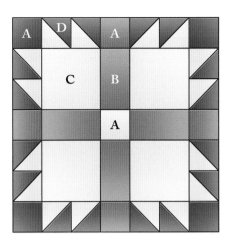

Bear's Paw

BEAR'S PAW

I was going to use a real bear for the background of this quilt, but I decided teddy bears would work better and be friendlier.

ADD ¼" SEAM ALLOWANCES TO YOUR
TEMPLATES BEFORE CUTTING.

10½" **FINISHED BLOCK**
Pieces in a fat quarter (18" x 20")
90 A
45 B
25 C
112 D

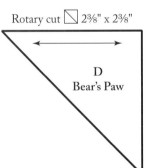

Rotary cut ◻ 2⅜" x 2⅜"

D
Bear's Paw

A
Bear's Paw

Rotary cut ◻ 2" x 2"

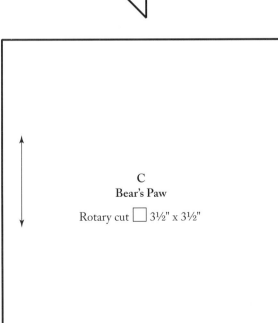

C
Bear's Paw

Rotary cut ◻ 3½" x 3½"

B
Bear's Paw

Rotary cut ▭ 2" x 3½"

Star in the Window

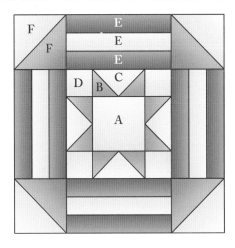

Star in the Window

ADD ¼" SEAM ALLOWANCES TO YOUR TEMPLATES BEFORE CUTTING.

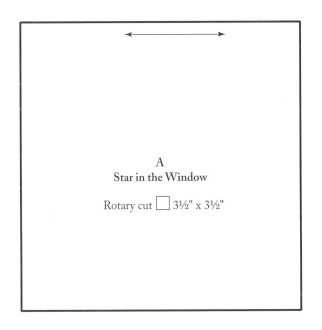

A
Star in the Window

Rotary cut ☐ 3½" x 3½"

12" FINISHED BLOCK
Pieces in a fat quarter (18" x 20")

25 A	90 D
112 B	36 E
64 C	40 F

Rotary cut ◺ 3⅞" x 3⅞"

F
Star in the Window

STAR IN THE WINDOW

I love the old quilts that have only two main colors. I thought the simple red and white quilt in this painting would help to anchor all the other textures.

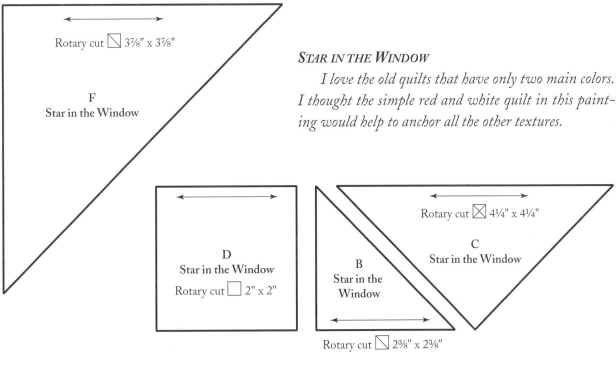

Rotary cut ⊠ 4¼" x 4¼"

C
Star in the Window

D
Star in the Window

Rotary cut ☐ 2" x 2"

B
Star in the Window

Rotary cut ◺ 2⅜" x 2⅜"

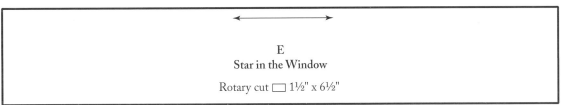

E
Star in the Window

Rotary cut ▭ 1½" x 6½"

Spools

This is a simple pattern but a lot of fun to do. I used a rainbow-type color scheme to give it harmony. Pattern on page 66.

Spools

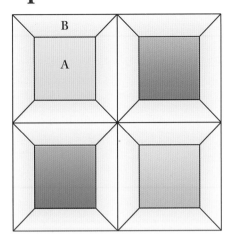

12" FINISHED BLOCK

Pieces in a fat quarter (18" x 20")

    20 A

    20 B

Quilt photo on pages 64 and 65.

ADD ¼" SEAM ALLOWANCES TO YOUR
TEMPLATES BEFORE CUTTING.

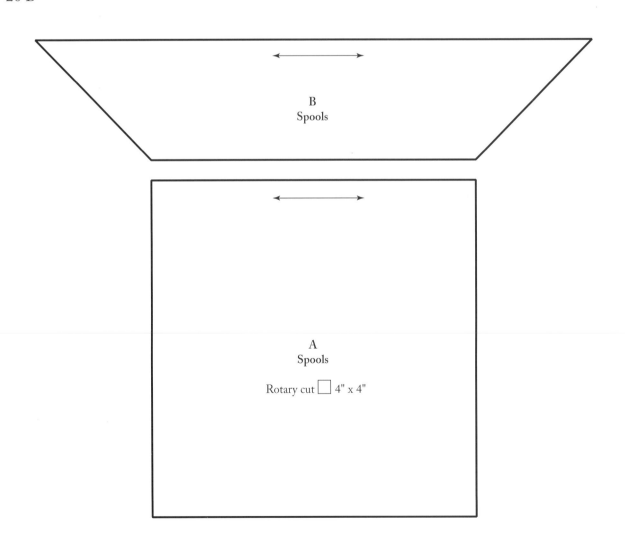

B
Spools

A
Spools

Rotary cut ⬜ 4" x 4"

Stars in the Field

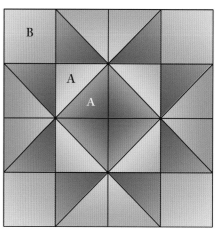

Quilt photo on pages 68 and 69.

12" FINISHED BLOCK
Pieces in a fat quarter (18" x 20")
    40 A
    25 B

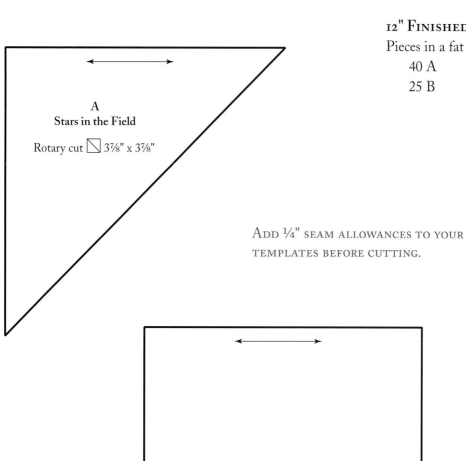

A
Stars in the Field

Rotary cut ◻ 3⅞" x 3⅞"

ADD ¼" SEAM ALLOWANCES TO YOUR
TEMPLATES BEFORE CUTTING.

B
Stars in the Field

Rotary cut ▢ 3½" x 3½"

Stars in the Field

This painting is dear to me. My family owned a dairy farm that had Holstein (black and white) cows. I consider them to be the stars in this field. Pattern on page 67.

Gallery

For your enjoyment, pages 70 through 76 provide a gallery of several more of Rebecca's charming paintings.

Amish

The Amish people are dear to my heart. I travel to Lancaster, Pennsylvania, every year for a quilt show, and after the show, I drive around to take pictures of the Amish farms to use in my paintings.

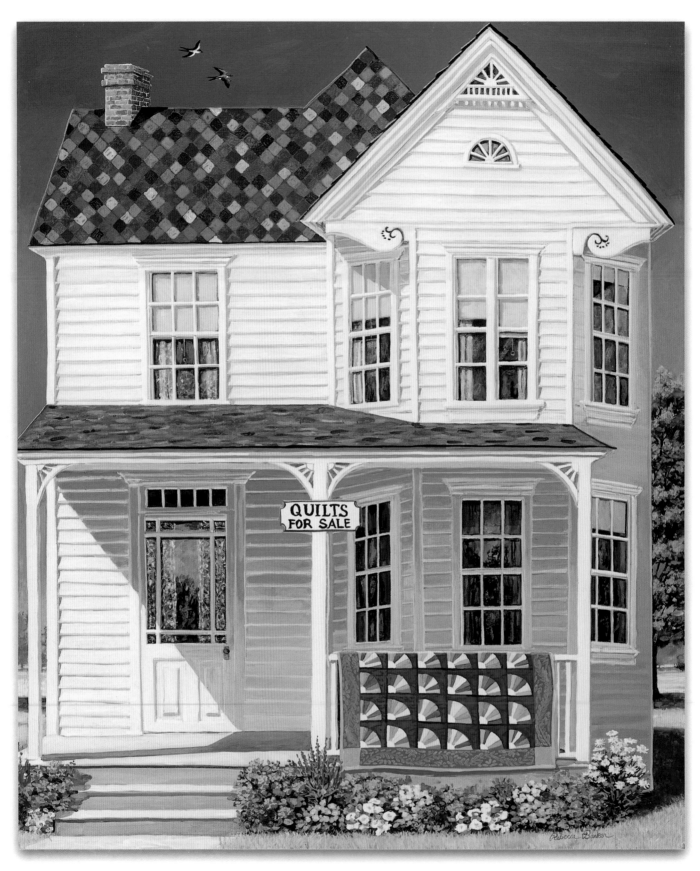

Quilts for Sale

The house in this painting was one I rented while in college. I always wanted to paint a picture of it for nostalgia.

Tulips

This tulip quiltscape features historically old tulip blocks. I tend to favor the older designs when picking out patterns.

Barn Raising

This painting was one of my first quiltscapes. When the light and dark fabrics in the
Log Cabin blocks form a diamond shape, the setting is called Barn Raising.

Flower Basket

I gave this painting variety by placing different flowers in every basket. This quilt also works well without the flowers.

Hawaiian Snowflake

Even though snow is a subject that does not come to my mind when I think of Hawaii,
I decided to use many cutwork snowflake designs and put a snow angel on top.

Bibliography

I thank the authors of the following books for their help in studying the quilt patterns I have selected to paint:

Aldrich, Margaret, editor. *Once Upon a Quilt.* Stillwater, MN: Voyageur Press, 2003.

Benberry, Cuesta Ray and Carol Pinney Crabb. *Love of Quilts.* Stillwater, MN: Voyageur Press, 2004.

Beyer, Jinny. *The Quilter's Album of Blocks and Borders.* Virginia: EPM Publications, 1986.

Brackman, Barbara. *Encyclopedia of Appliqué.* Virginia: EPM Publications, 1993.

_____. *Encyclopedia of Pieced Quilt Patterns.* Paducah, KY: American Quilter's Society, 1993.

Davis, Nancy. *The Baltimore Album Quilt Tradition.* Maryland Historical Society. Tokyo: Kokusai Art, 1999.

Hall, Carrie and Rose Kretsinger. *The Romance of the Patchwork Quilt.* New York: Dover Publishing, 1963.

Ickis, Marguerite. *The Standard Book of Quilt Making and Collecting.* New York: Dover Publishng, 1949.

Kelley, Helen. *Joy of Quilting.* Stillwater, MN: Voyageur Press, 2004.

Malone, Maggie. *5,500 Quilt Block Designs.* New York: Sterling Publishing Co., 2003.

Tree of Life

A small Tree of Life quilt hangs on the clothesline in this painting. The child is for youth and the grand-father for age and wisdom. A dead tree in the distance represents death, because it is very much a part of life.

Meet the Author

Art has always been a part of Rebecca's life. She grew up with paint and paper in hand, taking after her artist mother who painted Christmas ornaments. Aware of Rebecca's talent, her mother enrolled her in art classes at a very young age. Rebecca chose to pursue a degree in fine arts from Ohio University in Athens, and attended Miami University's Graduate Painting School in her hometown of Oxford, Ohio. Upon graduation, she decided that she couldn't make a living as a painter, so she began painting decorative decoy ducks. Seventeen years later, and in her early forties, Rebecca finally mustered up the confidence and courage she needed to return to painting pictures.

Growing up on her family's Oxford dairy farm, where quilting was a pastime for the Barker women, Rebecca developed a deep appreciation for quilts and the country landscape, so it was a natural progression for her landscape pictures to develop into "Quiltscapes." Rebecca has been working on this line of paintings since 1994 and has exhibited at national quilt shows, fine art shows, and on her web page. She has produced a line of note cards, limited edition prints, and many gift items.

Rebecca lives on the west side of Cincinnati in a quaint, old farmhouse, which also serves as her studio. She gets her quilt block patterns from quilt history books and quilt shows. "I do not make up the patterns. I love the designs of old quilts," she remarks. Once inspired, she creates her own color combinations and makes decisions about materials. She says, "My work is meant to honor the beauty of the old-time quilts and their makers."

Rebecca's beautiful paintings are available as notecards and limited edition prints. You can visit her Web site at www.barkerquiltscapes.com.

Other AQS Books

This is only a small selection of the books available from the American Quilter's Society. AQS books are known worldwide for timely topics, clear writing, beautiful color photos, and accurate illustrations and patterns. The following books are available from your local bookseller, quilt shop, or public library.

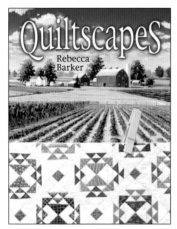

#6204   us$19.95

#6674   us$19.95

#6672   us$25.95

#6295   us$24.95

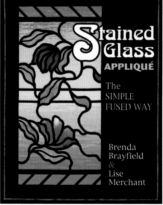

#6671   us$21.95

#6682   us$19.95

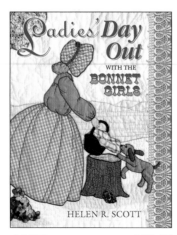

#6676   us$22.95

#5972   us$16.95

#6008   us$19.95

**Look for these books nationally.
Call or Visit our Web site at**

1-800-626-5420
www.AmericanQuilter.com